Mosquitoes

by Grace Hansen

ABDO
INSECTS
Kids

www.abdopublishing.com

Published by Abdo Kids, a division of ABDO, P.O. Box 398166, Minneapolis, Minnesota 55439.

Printed in the United States of America, North Mankato, Minnesota.

052014

092014

 THIS BOOK CONTAINS RECYCLED MATERIALS

Photo Credits: Shutterstock, Thinkstock

Production Contributors: Teddy Borth, Jennie Forsberg, Grace Hansen

Design Contributors: Candice Keimig, Laura Rask, Dorothy Toth

Library of Congress Control Number: 2013952312

Cataloging-in-Publication Data

Hansen, Grace.

 Mosquitoes / Grace Hansen.

  p. cm. -- (Insects)

ISBN 978-1-62970-041-0 (lib. bdg.)

Includes bibliographical references and index.

1. Mosquitoes--Juvenile literature.   I. Title.

595.77--dc23

2013952312

Table of Contents

Mosquitoes

Mosquitoes are insects.

Ants, bees, and beetles

are insects too.

5

Mosquitoes live almost

everywhere on Earth.

They are **often** found

near lakes and ponds.

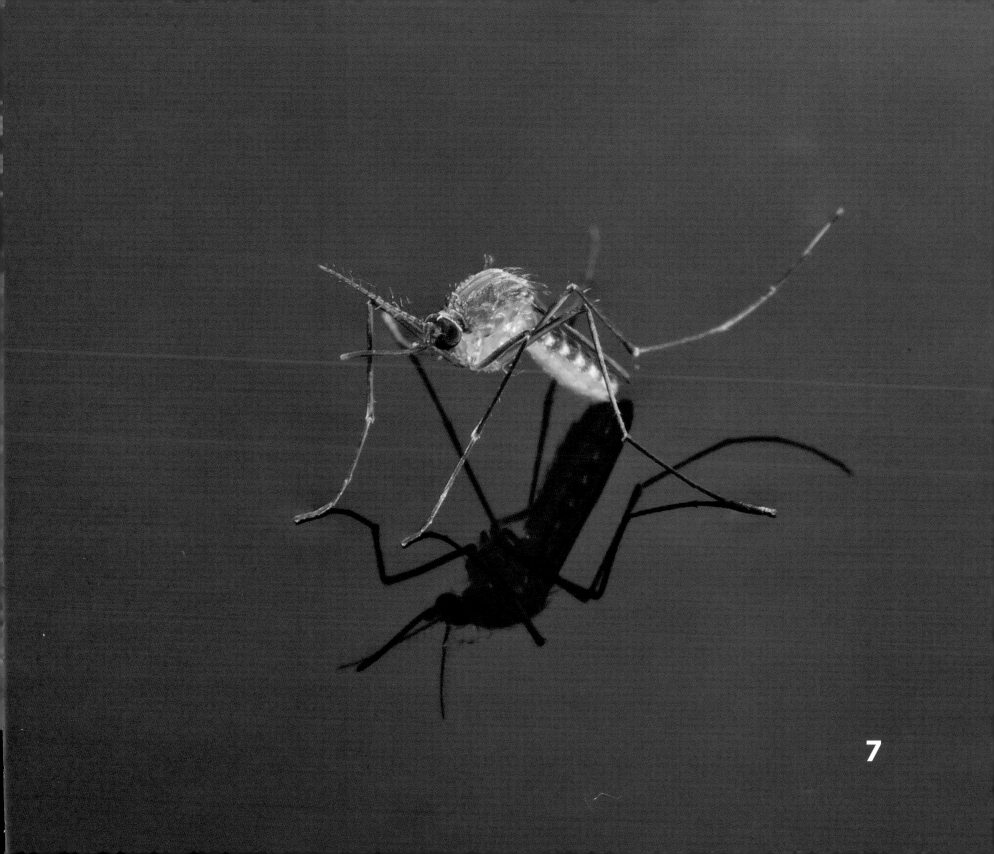

7

Most mosquitoes are

white, gray, or brown.

Some mosquitoes are

brightly colored.

Mosquitoes have three main body parts. They are the head, **thorax**, and the **abdomen**.

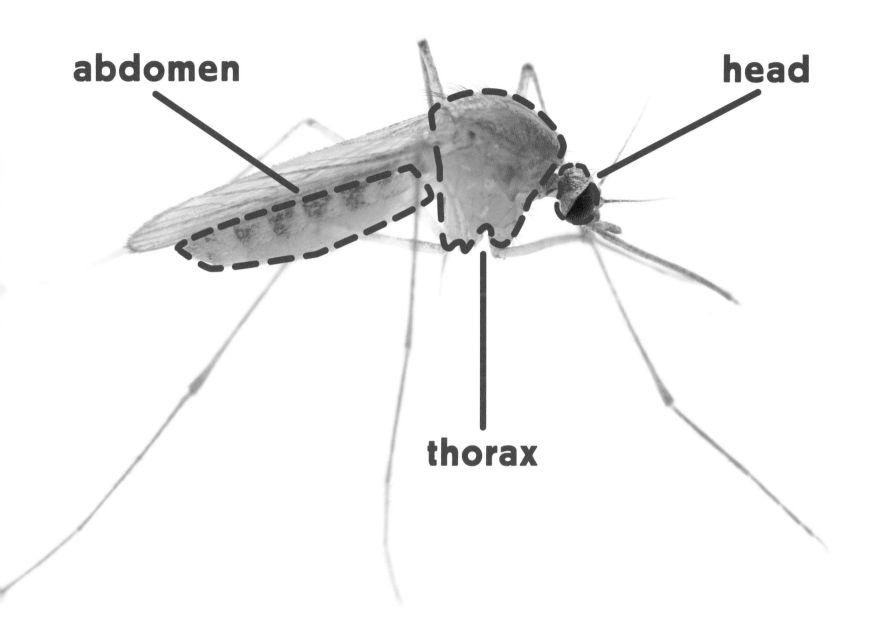

abdomen

head

thorax

Mosquitoes have six legs and two wings. They have two eyes and two antennae.

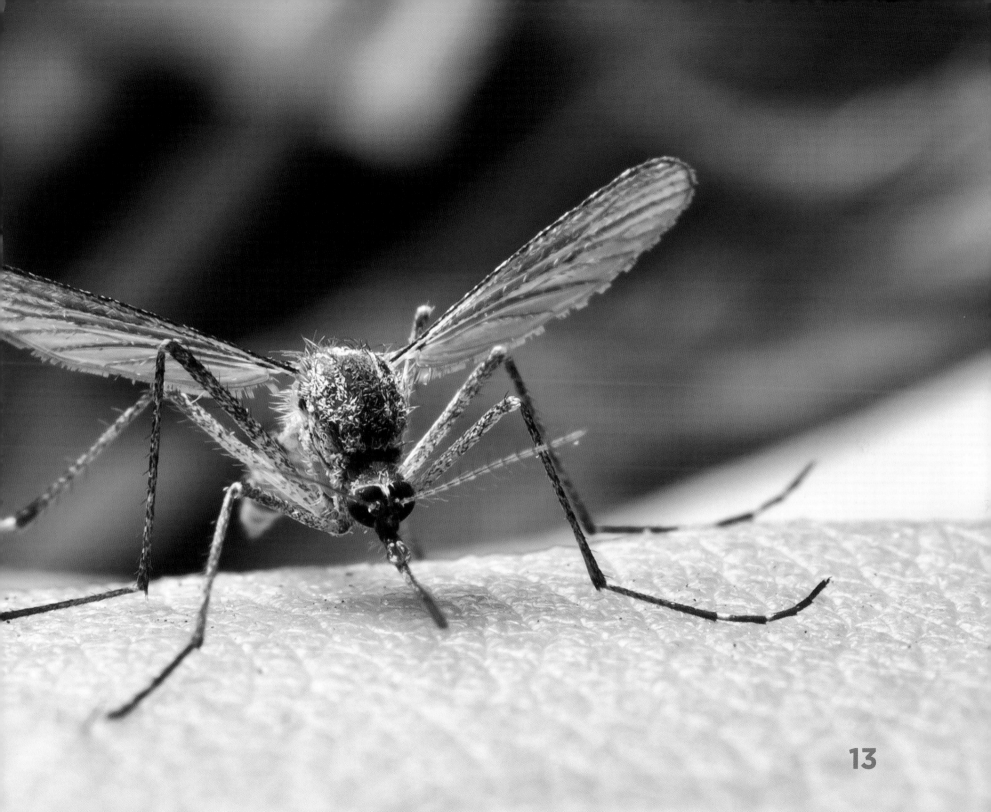

A mosquito has a
special **mouthpart**.
It looks like a straw.

14

Food

All mosquitoes eat

nectar and plant juices.

16

17

Only female mosquitoes

bite and drink blood. They

bite humans and animals.

Mosquitoes Help the Earth

Mosquitoes are important.
They are food for many
animals and other insects.

20

More Facts

- A mosquito's wings beat about 1,000 times per second. That is the buzzing sound you hear in your ear when they are around!

- There are more than 3,000 species of mosquitoes around the world.

- The word *mosquito* means "little fly" in Portuguese.

Glossary

abdomen – the back part of an insect's body.

mouthpart – a mouth shape that is for grasping, biting, or sucking.

nectar – a sweet liquid, or sugar water, that flowering plants make.

often – many times; usually.

thorax – the middle part of an insect's body.

Index

abdokids.com

Use this code to log on to abdokids.com and access crafts, games, videos and more!

Abdo Kids Code:
IMK0410